Andrew Murray
Believing Prayer

Andrew Murray
Believing Prayer

BETHANYHOUSE
Minneapolis, Minnesota

Believing Prayer
Andrew Murray

Copyright © 1980, 2004
Bethany House Publishers

Originally published under the titles *Have Faith in God*
and *In My Name* as two separate books.

Published by Bethany House in 1980 under the title
The Secret of Believing Prayer.

The 2004 edition has been revised and updated for today's reader.

Cover design by Eric Walljasper

Published by Bethany House Publishers
11400 Hampshire Avenue South
Bloomington, Minnesota 55438

Bethany House Publishers is a division of
Baker Publishing Group, Grand Rapids, Michigan.

Printed in the United States of America

Library of Congress Cataloging-in-Publication Data

Murray, Andrew, 1828–1917.
    Believing prayer / by Andrew Murray.
        p.   cm.
    Rev. and updated ed. of: The secret of believing prayer. 1980.
    ISBN 0–7642–2903–6 (pbk.)
    1. Prayer—Christianity. I. Murray, Andrew, 1828–1917. Secret of
believing prayer. II. Title.

BV210.3.M84   2004
    248.3'2—dc22   2004002184

ANDREW MURRAY was born in South Africa in 1828. After receiving his education in Scotland and Holland, he returned to South Africa and spent many years there as a missionary pastor. He was a staunch advocate of biblical Christianity, and is best known for his many devotional books. He and his wife, Emma, raised eight children.

BOOKS BY ANDREW MURRAY

FROM BETHANY HOUSE PUBLISHERS

With Updated Language

Abiding in Christ

Absolute Surrender

The Andrew Murray Daily Reader

The Believer's Daily Renewal

Believing Prayer

The Blood of Christ

Divine Healing

The Fullness of the Spirit

Humility

A Life of Obedience

Living a Prayerful Life

The Ministry of Intercessory Prayer

The Path to Holiness

Teach Me to Pray

Contents

Chapter 1

The Secret of Believing Prayer

*"Have faith in God," Jesus answered. "I tell you
the truth, if anyone says to this mountain, 'Go,
throw yourself into the sea,' and does not doubt
in his heart but believes that what he says will
happen, it will be done for him. Therefore I tell
you, whatever you ask for in prayer, believe that
you have received it, and it will be yours."*

Mark 11:22–24

The most wonderful promises in all of Scripture
are those regarding answers to prayer. To many,
such promises have raised the question, How can
I ever attain the faith that knows that it receives
all it asks?

It is this very question our Lord would answer
today. When He gave the above promise to His

disciples (vv. 23–24), He first pointed out where faith in the answer to prayer comes from and where it finds its strength: "Have faith in God" (v. 22). This command precedes the promise of answered prayer.

The power to believe a promise depends entirely on our faith in the one who promises. Trust in a person creates trust in his word. It is only when we enjoy a personal loving relationship with God himself that our whole being is opened up to the mighty influence of His holy presence and the capacity will be developed in us for believing that He gives whatever we ask.

The connection between faith in God and faith in His promises will become clear when we think about what faith really is. It is often compared to the hand or the mouth by which we take and appropriate what is offered to us. Faith is also the ear by which we hear what is promised, the eye by which we see what is offered. The power to take hold of something depends on this. I must *hear* the person who gives the promise— the very tone of his voice gives me courage to believe. I must *see* him—in the light of his eye and his countenance, all fear passes away. The value of the promise depends on the promiser;

my knowledge of the promiser's character and dependability creates faith in his promise.

For this reason, Jesus, when He gave that wonderful prayer-promise in Mark, first said, "Have faith in God." In other words, open your eyes to the living God, gaze on Him, and see Him who is invisible. Through my eyes I yield myself to the influence of what is before me; I allow it to enter my mind, to exert its influence and leave its impression on my heart. So believing God is simply looking to who He is, basking in His presence, yielding my whole being to take in the full impression of who He is, opening my soul to receive His love.

Yes, faith is the eye to which God reveals himself. Through faith, the light of His presence and the workings of His mighty power stream into the soul. As that which I see and behold lives in me, so by faith God lives in me.

Faith is also the ear through which the voice of God is heard and communication with Him is maintained. Through the Holy Spirit the Father speaks to us—the Spirit is the living voice; the Son is the Word, the substance of what God says. The child of God needs the voice from heaven to teach him what to say and do, just as it taught

Jesus. A believing heart and an ear opened toward God will hear Him speak.

The words of God will not only be the words of His Book, but proceeding from His mouth, words of spirit and truth, life and power. They will produce in deed and experience what would otherwise only be thoughts. Through an opened ear the soul tarries under the influence of the life and power of God himself. As the words I hear enter my mind and work their influence, so through faith God enters my heart and works His influence there.

When faith is in full exercise as eye and ear, the faculty of the soul by which we see and hear God, it will be able to exercise its full power as hand and mouth to appropriate God and His blessings. The power of reception will depend entirely on the power of our spiritual perception. For this reason Jesus said, "Have faith in God."

Faith is simply surrender: yielding ourselves to the impression of the words we hear. By faith we yield ourselves to the living God. His glory and love fill our hearts and have control over our lives. Faith is fellowship: it is giving ourselves over to the influence of a friend who makes a promise and in that way we become linked to that friend. When we enter into this living fellowship *with God himself,* in the faith that sees and hears Him, it becomes natural to believe His promises regarding prayer. Faith in the promise is the fruit of faith in the Promiser; the prayer of faith is rooted in the life of faith.

In this way, the faith that prays effectually is a gift of God. Not as something that He bestows or infuses but as the blessed disposition or habit of soul that is wrought in a life of communion with Him. Surely for one who knows his Father well and lives in constant close fellowship with Him, it is a simple thing to believe the promise that He will do the will of His child.

Because many of God's children do not understand this connection between the life of faith and the prayer of faith, their experience of the power of prayer is very limited. When they desire to obtain an answer from God, they fix their whole heart upon the promise and try their utmost to grasp it in faith. When they do not succeed, they give up hope; the promise is true, but it is beyond their power to take hold of it. Listen to the lesson Jesus teaches us: "Have faith in God"—the living God. Let faith look to God more than the thing promised; His love, His power, His living presence will awaken and work out real faith.

To one who asks for the means to gain strength in his arms and hands, a physician would say that his whole body must be built up and strengthened. So the cure for weak faith is found in the building up of one's whole spiritual life by communing with God. Learn to believe God, to take hold of Him, to let Him take possession of your life; then it will be easy to take hold of the promise. He who knows and trusts God finds it easy to trust the promise as well.

Notice how evident this was in the saints of old. Every special exhibition of the power of faith was the fruit of a special revelation of God. See it in the case of Abraham: "After this, the word of the LORD came to Abram in a vision: 'Do not be afraid, Abram. I am your shield, your very great reward. . . .' He also said to him, 'I am the LORD, who brought you out of Ur of the Chaldeans to give you this land to take possession of it'" (Genesis 15:1, 7). After further revelation concerning his offspring and the land he would possess, Abram believed the Lord.

In a later instance when the Lord appeared to him, Abram fell facedown and laughed, such was the incredible nature of God's revelation to him. But it was the revelation of God himself that gave the promise living power to enter Abraham's heart and to build his faith.

Because he knew God, Abraham could only trust His promise. God's promise will be to us what God himself is to us. It is the man who walks before the Lord, and even falls on his face to listen while God speaks to him, who will receive the promise. Though we have God's promises in the Bible, with full liberty to appropriate them, spiritual power is lacking until God himself speaks them to us. And He speaks to those who walk and live with Him.

Therefore, let your faith be all eyes and ears. Surrender to God; allow Him to make His full impression and reveal himself fully in your soul. Count it one of the chief blessings of prayer to exercise faith in God—the living mighty God who waits to fulfill in us all the good pleasure of His will. See Him as the God of love, who delights to bless us and impart himself to us. As we worship God, power will come to believe the promise: "Whatever you ask for in prayer, believe that you have received it, and it will be yours" (Mark 11:24). As in faith you make God your own, the promise will be yours as well.

We naturally seek God's gifts, but God wants to give us himself first. We think of prayer as the power that brings down the good gifts of heaven, and Jesus as the means to draw us up to God. We tend to stand at the door and cry out our request, but Jesus would have us enter in and realize that we are friends and children.

Let every experience of the smallness of your faith in prayer encourage you to have and exercise more faith in the living God. A heart that is full of God has power for the prayer of faith. Faith in God gives birth to faith in the promise— the promise of answered prayer.

Therefore, as children of God, let us take time to bow before Him, to wait on Him to reveal himself to us. Take the time necessary to let your soul exercise and express its faith in your all-powerful God. As He imparts himself to you and takes possession of you, the prayer of faith will emerge.

O God, I do truly believe in you. I believe you are my Father; I believe in your infinite love and power. I believe in your Son, my Redeemer and my life. And I believe in your Holy Spirit, my

Comforter, Guide, and strength. Three-in-One God, I have faith in you. I know and am certain that all you are you are to me, that all you have promised you will perform.

Lord Jesus, increase my faith. Teach me to take time to wait and worship in your holy presence until my faith appropriates all there is in you for me. Let me see you as the fountain of life, working with your mighty strength to accomplish your will in the world and in me. Let me see your love that is longing to meet and fulfill all my desires. Let your love so take possession of my heart and life that through faith I will know you dwelling in me. Lord Jesus, help me, that with my whole heart I might believe in you. Let my faith in you fill me every moment.

My blessed Savior, how can your church glorify you? How can it fulfill the work of intercession, through which your kingdom must come, unless our whole life is filled with faith in God? Blessed Lord, speak your Word, "Have faith in God," into the depths of my soul. Amen.

Chapter 2

The Cure for Unbelief

Then the disciples came to Jesus in private and asked, "Why couldn't we drive it out?" He replied, "Because you have so little faith. I tell you the truth, if you have faith as small as a mustard seed, you can say to this mountain, 'Move from here to there' and it will move. Nothing will be impossible for you."

Matthew 17:19–20

"However, this kind does not go out except by prayer and fasting."

Matthew 17:21 NKJV

When the disciples saw Jesus cast the evil spirit out of the epileptic boy whom "they could not heal" (v. 16), they asked the Master for the cause of their failure. He had given them power and authority over all demons and diseases. They had often exercised that power, and joyfully told how the demons were subject to them. Yet now, while He was on the Mount, they had utterly failed.

There had been nothing in the will of God or in the nature of the case to render deliverance impossible—at Christ's bidding the evil spirit had gone out. From their question "Why couldn't we drive it out?" it is evident that they had wished and tried to do so; they had probably used the Master's name and commanded the evil spirit to leave. Their efforts had been in vain, however, and in front of the multitude, they had been put to shame.

Christ's answer was direct and plain: "Because you have so little faith." Their failure was not due to some special power that was unavailable to them. He had often taught them that there is one power—that of faith—to which everything in the kingdom of darkness and in the kingdom of God must bow; in the spiritual world, failure has but one cause: lack of faith.

Faith is the one condition on which divine power can enter a person and work through him. It is the will of a person yielded to and molded by the will of God. The power the disciples received to cast out demons was not a power they held in themselves as a permanent gift or possession; rather, it was the power of Christ, to be received and used by faith alone. Had they been full of faith in Him as Lord and Conqueror of the spirit-world, full of faith in Him as having given them authority to cast out demons in His name, they would have had the victory. Little faith or unbelief was the Master's perennial explanation and reproof of a lack of power or failure in His church.

Lack of faith must have a cause. The disciples might have asked, Why couldn't we believe? We have cast out demons before. What happened this time?

The Master told them, "This kind does not go out except by prayer and fasting" (Matthew 17:21 NKJV). While faith may be the simplest, it is also the highest exercise of the spiritual life, where one's spirit yields itself in perfect receptivity to God's Spirit, and is thus strengthened to its highest degree. This faith depends entirely upon the state of the spiritual life; only when this is strong and in full health, when the Spirit of God has full sway in one's life, is there the power of faith to do mighty acts. This is why Jesus added, "except by prayer and fasting."

Jesus was telling them, The faith that can overcome such stubborn resistance as you have seen in this evil spirit is not possible except to those living in very close fellowship with God and in very special separation from the world—in prayer and fasting. Therefore, He teaches us two lessons in regard to prayer: (1) faith needs a life of prayer in which to grow and remain strong; and (2) prayer needs fasting for its full and perfect development.

Faith needs a life of prayer for its full growth. In all the various aspects of the spiritual life, there is such union, such unceasing action and reaction, that each may be both cause and effect. And so it is with faith. There can be no true prayer without faith; some measure of faith must precede prayer. Yet prayer is also the way to more faith; there can be no higher degree of faith except through more prayer.

Nothing needs to grow so much as our faith. "Your faith is growing more and more" is said of one church (2 Thessalonians 1:3). When Jesus spoke the words "According to your faith will it be done to you" (Matthew 9:29), He announced the law of the kingdom, which tells us that not all have equal degrees of faith, that the same person does not always have the same degree, and that the measure of faith determines the measure of power and of blessing.

If we want to know where and how our faith is to grow, the Master points us to the throne of God. It is in prayer, the exercise of faith in fellowship with the living God, that faith can increase. Faith can live only as it is nurtured by God himself.

It is in the worship of God, the deep silence of soul that yields itself to God that He might reveal himself, that our capacity for knowing and trusting God will be developed. It is as we take His Word, bringing it before Him, asking Him to make it living and real to us, that the power will come to fully believe it and receive it as our own. It is in prayer, in living contact with the living God, that faith to trust God and to accept all that He says will become real to us.

Many Christians do not understand what is meant by the "much prayer" they hear spoken of; they have no concept, nor do they feel the need, of spending extended periods of time with God. But the experience of His people confirms the fact that men and women of strong faith are men and women of much prayer.

This brings us back to the lesson of the first chapter: "Have faith in God." It is God, the living God, in whom our faith must plant its roots deep and broad; then it will be strong enough to remove mountains and cast out devils: "If you have faith . . . nothing will be impossible for you" (Matthew 17:20).

If we would commit ourselves to the work God has for us in the world, coming into contact with the mountains and the demons that must be brought down and cast out, we would soon comprehend the need for much faith and much prayer—the soil in which faith can be cultivated. Christ Jesus is not only our life, He is the life of our faith. It is His life in us that makes us strong enough and simple enough to believe.

The spirit of faith will come in power when we die to self—a necessary condition for much prayer and closer union with Jesus.

Prayer also needs fasting for its full growth. Prayer is the one hand with which we grasp the invisible; fasting, the other, with which we let go of and cast away the visible. In nothing is man more closely connected with the world of sense than in his need for food and his enjoyment of it. It was the fruit, good for food, with which man was tempted in the Garden. It was with bread to be made of stones that Jesus, when hungry, was tempted in the wilderness; in fasting He triumphed.

The body has been redeemed to be a temple of the Holy Spirit; in body as well as spirit, but especially, Scripture says, in eating and drinking, we are to glorify God. There are many Christians to whom eating to the glory of God has not yet become a spiritual reality.

The first thought suggested by Jesus' words in regard to fasting and prayer is that only in a life of moderation, temperance, and self-denial will there be the heart or the strength to pray at length.

There is also its more literal meaning: Sorrow and anxiety cannot eat; joy celebrates its feasts with eating and drinking. There may come times of intense desire when it seems obvious that the body, with its appetites, lawful though they be, still hinder the spirit in its battle with the powers of darkness; the need is felt of keeping the body under.

We are creatures of the senses; our mind is helped by what comes to us embodied in concrete form; fasting helps to express, to deepen, and to confirm the resolution that we are ready to sacrifice anything—even ourselves—to attain what we seek for the kingdom of God. He who accepted the fasting and sacrifice of the Son values, accepts, and rewards with spiritual power the soul that is thus ready to give up all for Christ and His kingdom.

There follows a still wider application. Prayer is the reaching out after God and the unseen; fasting, the letting go of all that is seen and temporal. Ordinary Christians imagine that all that is not positively forbidden and sinful is lawful to them, and they seek to retain as much as possible of this world, with its goods, entertainment, and creature comforts. But the truly consecrated soul is a soldier who carries only what he needs for warfare. Laying aside every weight, as well as the sin that comes easily to him, afraid of entangling himself with the affairs of this life, he seeks to lead a life of one who is specially set apart for the Lord and His service. Without such voluntary separation, even from what is lawful, no one will attain real power in prayer.

You who are disciples of Jesus and have asked the Master to teach you to pray, accept the lessons He gives. He tells you prayer is the path to faith, a strong faith that can cast out demons. He tells us if we have faith, nothing will be impossible to us. Let this glorious promise be an encouragement to spend more time in prayer.

Is the prize not worth the price? Will you give up all to follow Jesus in the path He opens up to you? Will you fast when you feel it is necessary? Will you refrain from anything that hinders you in your life work—that of communing with God in prayer that you might become a person of faith whom He can use in His work of saving the world?

Lord Jesus, how continually you have to reprove me for my unbelief! How strange it must appear to you, this awful incapacity of trusting my Father and His promises. Lord, let your reproof sink into the very depths of my heart and reveal to me how much of the sin and suffering around me could be alleviated if I would but pray. And then teach me, blessed Lord, that there is a place where faith can be learned and gained—in the place of prayer and fasting that brings me into living and abiding fellowship with you and with the Father.

O Savior, you are the author and the perfecter of my faith; teach me what it is to allow you to live in me by your Holy Spirit. Lord, my efforts and prayers for grace to believe have been unavailing. And I know why; I sought for strength in myself. Dear Jesus, teach me the mystery of your life in me, and how you, by your Spirit, undertake to live in me the life of faith, to see to it that my faith shall not fail. Let me see how my faith can be a part of that wonderful prayer life that you give to those who expect their training for the ministry of intercession to come not in word and thought alone, but in the anointing of the Holy Spirit. And teach me how, in fasting and prayer, I may grow into the faith to which nothing is impossible. Amen.

Chapter 3

The Relationship of Prayer and Love

"And when you stand praying, if you hold anything against anyone, forgive him, so that your Father in heaven may forgive you your sins."

Mark 11:25

These words immediately follow the great prayer promise, "Whatever you ask for in prayer, believe that you have received it, and it will be yours" (v. 24). We have already seen how the words that preceded our promise "Have faith in God" show that in prayer everything depends upon our relationship to God being clear. The words that follow it remind us that our relationship with others must also be unhindered. Love for God and love for our neighbor are inseparable; prayer from a

— 31 —

heart that either is not right with God or that cannot get along with others can have no real effect. Faith and love are interdependent.

This is something that our Lord frequently emphasized. In the Sermon on the Mount (Matthew 5:23–24), when speaking of the sixth commandment, He taught His disciples that acceptable worship of the Father was not possible unless everything was right with a brother: "Therefore, if you are offering your gift at the altar and there remember that your brother has something against you, leave your gift there in front of the altar. First go and be reconciled to your brother; then come and offer your gift."

When speaking of prayer to God, after having taught us to pray, "Forgive us our debts, as we also have forgiven our debtors," Jesus added at the close of the prayer, "If you do not forgive men their sins, your Father will not forgive your sins" (Matthew 6:9–15).

At the close of the parable of the unmerciful servant, Jesus applies His teaching in the words: "This is how my heavenly Father will treat each of you unless you forgive your brother from your heart."

Standing beside the dried-up fig tree, where

Jesus speaks of the wonderful power of faith and the prayer of faith, He all at once, apparently without connection, introduces the thought, "And when you stand praying, if you hold anything against anyone, forgive him, so that your Father in heaven may forgive you your sins." It seems the Lord had learned during His life on earth that to men, disobedience to the law of love was the greatest sin, even of praying people, and no doubt the cause of the weakness of their prayers. It seems He wanted to lead us into His own experience: that nothing gives such liberty of access and such power in believing as the consciousness that we have given ourselves in love and compassion for those whom God loves.

The first lesson taught here is our need for a disposition of forgiveness. The Scripture admonishes us to forgive one another as God, for Christ's sake, has forgiven us. God's full and free forgiveness is the standard for our forgiveness. If we are reluctant or halfhearted about it, which is not forgiveness at all, neither will God forgive us.

Every prayer depends upon our faith in God's pardoning grace. If God dealt with us according to our sins, not one prayer would be heard. Pardon opens the door to all of God's love and blessing; because God has pardoned our sins, our prayers can prevail. The ground for answered prayer is God's forgiving love. When God's love and forgiveness have taken possession of our hearts, we will pray in faith and we will live in love. God's forgiving disposition, revealed in His love to us, will become our disposition as the power of His forgiving love is shed abroad in our hearts.

If a great injury or injustice is done to us, we must seek first of all to maintain a godlike disposition—to be kept from a desire to maintain our rights or to punish the offender as he deserves. In the annoyances of daily life, we must be careful not to excuse a hasty temper, sharp words, or rash judgment by saying that we meant no harm, that we did not hold the anger long, or that it is too much to ask of a weak human nature not to behave in such a manner. Instead, we must seek to forgive as God in Christ has forgiven us, and thus diffuse the anger and the judgment.

The blood that cleanses our conscience from dead works (works without faith) also cleanses from selfishness; the love it reveals is a pardoning love that takes possession of us and flows through us to others. Our forgiving love to others is the evidence of God's forgiving love in us and therefore the condition of the prayer of faith.

There is a second, more general lesson: Our daily life in the world comprises the rest of our communion with God in prayer. Often when a Christian comes to pray, he does his utmost to cultivate a certain frame of mind that he thinks will please God. He misunderstands, or forgets, that our daily life is the large part of our communion with God. How we are in everyday circumstances is how God sees us.

Life is a whole, and God judges the pious frame of the hour of prayer according to the ordinary frame of the daily life—of which the hour of prayer is but a small part. The tone of my life during the day, not the frame of mind I conjure up, is God's criterion of what I am and what I desire. My drawing nigh to God is integral to my relationship to others on earth; failure here will cause failure there. This occurs not only when there is the distinct consciousness of something wrong between my neighbor and me, but the unloving thoughts and words I allow to pass unnoticed can also hinder my prayer.

The effectual prayer of faith is the direct result of a life given up to the will and the love of

God. My prayer is heard by God not according to what I try to be when I am praying, but who I am when I am not praying.

There is also a third lesson: In our interaction with others every day, the one thing on which everything depends is love. The spirit of forgiveness is the spirit of love. Because God is love, He forgives; it is only when we are dwelling in His love that we can forgive others. Love of the brethren is evidence of our love of the Father, our ground of confidence before God and the assurance that our prayers will be heard (1 John 3:18–21, 23; 4:20). Neither faith nor work will profit if we have no love; it is love that proves the reality of faith. As essential as the condition that precedes the great prayer-promise in Mark 11:24—"Have faith in God"—is the one that follows it: Have love toward others. A right relationship to the living God and to the living men and women around me every day are the conditions of effectual prayer.

This love is of special consequence when we work among people and pray for them. We sometimes give ourselves to work for Christ from zeal for His cause, or for our own spiritual health, without giving ourselves in self-sacrificing love for those whose souls we seek to save. It is no wonder our faith is weak and ineffectual. We must look on each person, however undesirable, in the light of the tender love of Jesus the Shepherd seeking the lost—this is the secret of believing and successful prayer.

Jesus, in speaking of forgiveness, calls love its root. In the Sermon on the Mount He couples His teaching and promises about prayer with the call to be merciful as He is merciful (Matthew 5:7, 38–48). We also see it here: A loving life is the condition of believing prayer.

It has been said, There is nothing so heart-searching as believing prayer, or even the honest effort to pray in faith. Do not avoid the edge of that self-examination by the thought that God does not hear prayer for reasons known only to himself. This is not true. If we don't receive what we ask, we must examine our prayer and our motives. Let the Word of God search us. Let us ask ourselves whether our prayer is the expression of a life wholly given over to the will of God and the love of our fellowmen.

Love is the only soil in which faith can take root and thrive. As it reaches heavenward, the Father looks to see if it reaches equally to the evil and the unworthy as well as to the kind and deserving.

He who allows the love of God to dwell in him, and in the practice of daily life purposes to love as God loves, will have reason to believe that his prayers are heard. It is *the Lamb* who is in the midst of the throne; it is forbearing love that prevails with God in prayer. The merciful shall obtain mercy; the meek shall inherit the earth.

Blessed Father, you are Love. Only those who abide in love abide in you and in fellowship with you. The Son has taught me again how deeply true this is of my fellowship with you in prayer. O God, let your love, shed abroad in my heart by the Holy Spirit, be in me a fountain of love to all those around me so that out of my life may spring the power of believing prayer. Grant that this may be my experience by the Holy Spirit: a life lived in your love to all around me is key. Help me to find the power of forgiveness and the joy that is found in readily forgiving any and all who might offend me.

Lord Jesus, my blessed teacher, teach me to freely forgive and to love as you do. Let the power of your blood make the pardon of my sins such a reality that forgiveness will come naturally and freely. Show me whatever hinders my fellowship with you, so that my daily life in my home and in society may be the school in which strength and confidence are gathered for the prayer of faith. Amen.

Chapter 4

The Power of United Prayer

*"Again, I tell you that if two of you on earth
agree about anything you ask for, it will be done
for you by my Father in heaven. For where two
or three come together in my name,
there am I with them."*

Matthew 18:19–20

One of the first lessons our Lord taught in His
school of prayer was the importance of not being
seen of men. He was speaking of the need for private prayer between you and God alone. The second lesson with regard to prayer is that we need
not only secret prayer but also public, united
prayer.

Our Scripture gives us a very special promise
for the united prayer of two or three who agree

about what they are asking. Just as a tree's root is hidden in the ground and its stem and leaf grow toward the sunlight, so prayer needs for its full development the secrecy in which the soul meets God alone as well as the public fellowship with those who in the name of Jesus find a common meeting place.

The bond that unites a person with fellow Christians is no less real and close than that which unites him to God—he is one with them. Grace renews not only our relationship to God but also to others. We learn to say not only *my* Father but *our* Father. Nothing would be more unnatural than for a child of a family to always meet with his father separately and never together with his mother and siblings.

Believers are members not only of one family but of one body. Each member of the body depends on the others, and the full working of the spirit dwelling in the body depends on the union and cooperation of all. So also, Christians cannot reach the full blessing God wants to bestow through His Spirit unless they seek and receive it in fellowship with one another. In the union and fellowship of believers, the Spirit can manifest His full power. It was to the 120 continuing in one place together and praying with one accord that the Spirit manifested himself.

The marks of genuine united prayer are given to us in our Scripture for this chapter. The *first* mark is *agreement* as to the thing asked. There must not only be general consent on what is asked, but there must also be a distinct united desire for it. The agreement must be, as in all prayer, in spirit and in truth. When we are agreed, it will become clear to us exactly what we are asking, so that we may be confident that we are asking according to God's will and therefore may believe that we have received what we ask.

The *second* mark of united prayer is *gathering in the name of Jesus*. Here our Lord teaches that His name must be the center of the union in which believers gather, the bond that makes them one, just as a home contains and unites all who are in it. The name of the Lord is a strong tower; the righteous run into it and are safe.

That name is such a reality to those who understand its authority and believe in it, that to meet in His name is to have Jesus present. The love and unity of His disciples have an infinite attraction to Jesus: "For where two or three come

together in my name, there am I with them"
(Matthew 18:20). The living presence of Jesus in
the fellowship of His loving, praying disciples
gives united prayer its power.

The *third* mark of united prayer is *the certain
answer:* "It will be done for you by my Father in
heaven" (v. 19). A prayer meeting for maintaining Christian fellowship or seeking personal edi-
fication may have its place, but this was not the
Lord's primary purpose in instituting it. He
meant it to be a means of securing *answers to
prayer.*

A prayer meeting without recognized answers
to prayer ought to be an anomaly. When any of
us has a distinct desire or request for which we
feel too weak to exercise the necessary faith, we
ought to seek the strength and help of others. In
the unity of faith, love, and the power of the
Spirit, the presence of Christ and the certainty of
an answer are promised. The evidence of true
united prayer is its fruit: the answer—receiving
what we have asked for.

United prayer is a great privilege, and its
power waits to be experienced. If the believing
couple knew they were joined together in the
name of Jesus to experience His presence and

power in united prayer; if friends believed how effective two or three praying in concert could be; if in every prayer meeting faith in His presence and expectation of an answer were foremost; if in every church united prayer was regarded as one of the chief purposes for which Christians come together—the highest exercise of their power as a church; if in the church universal the coming of the kingdom, and the King himself, first in the mighty outpouring of His Holy Spirit, and then in His own glorious person, were matters of ceaseless pleading with God, who could predict what blessing might come through those who agree to prove God's promises?

The apostle Paul is a great example of faith in the power of united prayer. To the Romans he writes (15:30): "I urge you, brothers, by our Lord Jesus Christ and by the love of the Spirit, to join me in my struggle by praying to God for me." He expected to be delivered from his enemies and to prosper in his work.

In his second letter to the Corinthians he declared (1:11), ". . . as you help us by your prayers. Then many will give thanks on our behalf for the gracious favor granted us in answer to the prayers of many." Their prayer was to have a significant share in his deliverance. Of the Ephesians he requested, "And pray in the Spirit on all occasions with all kinds of prayers and requests... always keep on praying for all the saints. Pray also for me, that whenever I open my mouth, words may be given me so that I will fearlessly make known the mystery of the gospel" (6:18–19). Power and success in his ministry depended on their prayers.

Paul informed the Philippians (1:19) that he expected his trials would turn to his salvation and the progress of the gospel, "for I know that through your prayers and the help given by the Spirit of Jesus Christ, what has happened to me will turn out for my deliverance." He challenged the Colossians (4:3) to continue steadfast in prayer, "and pray for us, too, that God may open a door for our message, so that we may proclaim the mystery of Christ."

Paul urged the Thessalonians in his second letter (3:1), "Finally, brothers, pray for us that the message of the Lord may spread rapidly and be honored, just as it was with you." It is evident that Paul considered himself part of a body, dependent on the sympathy and cooperation of each member; he counted on the prayers of the churches to see his work go forward. The prayers of the church were to him as significant in the work of the kingdom as the power of God.

Who can say what power a church could experience if it gave itself to prayer day and night for the coming of the kingdom, for God's power on His servants and His Word, for the glory of God in the salvation of souls? Most churches think their members are brought together to take care of one another and build each other up. Often they are unaware of the fact that God rules the world by the prayers of His saints, that prayer is the power by which Satan is conquered, and that by prayer the church on earth has authority over the powers of the spirit world. They do not fully realize, if they know it at all, that Jesus has by His promise consecrated every assembly in His name to be a gate of heaven, where His presence is felt and His power is experienced.

There will be untold blessing when God's people meet as one in the name of Jesus to know His presence and boldly claim the promise that the Father will do what they agree to ask.

Blessed Lord, you asked in your high-priestly prayer for the unity of your people. Show us how you invite us to this unity by your promises concerning united prayer. It is when we are one in love and desire that our faith knows your presence and the Father's answer.

Father, we do pray for your people, and for every smaller circle of those who meet together, that they may be one in you. Remove all selfishness and self-interest, all narrowness of heart and estrangement by which unity is hindered. Cast out the spirit of the world and the flesh through which your promises lose their power. Let the thought of your presence and the Father's favor draw us closer to each other.

Grant, blessed Lord, that your church might learn and believe that it is by the power of united prayer that she can accomplish great things for your kingdom; that Satan can be cast out; that souls can be saved; that mountains can be removed; that the kingdom can be brought nearer. And grant, dear Lord, that in the circle in which we pray, the prayer of the church may indeed be the power through which your name and your Word are uplifted and glorified. Amen.

— *Chapter 5* —

The Power of
Persevering Prayer

*Then Jesus told his disciples a parable to show
them that they should always pray and not give
up. . . . "Listen to what the unjust judge says.
And will not God bring about justice for his
chosen ones, who cry out to him day and night?
Will he keep putting them off? I tell you, he will
see that they get justice, and quickly."*

Luke 18:1–3

One of the greatest mysteries of prayer is the
need for perseverance. That our loving Lord, so
longing to bless, should have to be sought time
after time, sometimes year after year, before the
answer comes, is not easy to understand. It is also
one of the greatest practical difficulties in the exercise of believing prayer. When after persevering

supplication our prayer remains unanswered, it is often easiest for our pampered flesh (and it has all the appearance of pious submission) to think that we must stop praying because God may have a reason for withholding His answer.

By faith alone the difficulty is overcome. When faith has taken its stand on God's Word and in the name of Jesus, and has yielded itself to the leading of the Spirit to seek only God's will and honor in its prayer, it need not be discouraged by delay. It knows from Scripture that the power of believing prayer is simply irresistible; *real faith can never be disappointed*. Just as the flow of a great amount of water creates an accumulated pressure, there must often be a heaping up of prayer until God sees that the measure is full, and the answer comes. Faith knows that just as the farmer must take ten thousand steps and sow ten thousand seeds in preparation for the final harvest, so there is a need for oft-repeated, persevering prayer in order to receive a desired blessing. Faith knows that not a single believing prayer fails to have its effect in heaven; each has influence and is treasured up to work out an answer in due time to him who perseveres to the end.

Faith does not depend on human thoughts or possibilities but on the Word of the living God. Even as Abraham through so many years in hope believed against hope, and then through faith *and patience* inherited the promise, faith believes that the long-suffering of the Lord is salvation, *waiting* and *pressing on* unto the coming of its Lord to fulfill His promise.

Try to understand the two words in which our Lord sets forth the character and conduct not of the unjust judge but of our God and Father toward those whom He allows to cry day and night to Him: "He will see that they get justice, and quickly." This will enable you, when the answer to your prayer does not come at once, to combine quiet patience and joyful confidence in your persevering prayer.

The blessing is all prepared; He is not only willing but eager to give what we ask; everlasting love burns with the desire to reveal itself fully to His beloved and to satisfy her needs. God will not delay one moment longer than is absolutely necessary. He will do all in His power to hasten the answer.

But if this is true, and His power is infinite, why must we often wait so long for the answer to prayer? And why must God's own elect, so often in the midst of suffering and conflict, plead day and night? He is *long-suffering*. The farmer longs for his harvest, but knows that it must have its full season of sunshine and rain, so he waits patiently. A child so often wants to pick the half-ripe fruit; the farmer will wait for the proper time.

We, in our spiritual nature, are also under the law of gradual growth that controls all created life. Only by proper development can we reach our divine destiny. It is the Father, in whose hands are the times and seasons, who alone knows the moment when the soul or the church is ripened to that fullness of faith in which it can receive and secure the blessing. As a mother who longs to have her only child home from school, and yet waits patiently until the time of training is completed, so it is with God and His children; He is the long-suffering One, and answers in a timely fashion.

Recognition of this truth leads the believer to cultivate the corresponding dispositions: *patience, faith, hope,* and *endurance* are the secrets of perseverance. By faith in the promises of God, we know that we *have* the petitions we have asked of Him. Faith takes hold of the answer as an unseen spiritual possession; faith rejoices in it and gives thanks for it as though it already has it.

But there is a difference between the faith that believes the word and knows it has the answer and the clearer, fuller, riper faith that obtains the promise as a present experience. It is in persevering, confident, thankful prayer that the soul grows up into full union with its Lord so that it can experience possession of the blessing.

There may be from God's viewpoint people and situations that have to be put right before the answer to our prayer can fully come. The faith that according to the command believes that it has already received can allow God to take all the time He needs. In quiet, persistent, and determined perseverance it continues in prayer and thanksgiving until the blessing comes. The combination appears contradictory: the faith that rejoices in the answer of the unseen God as a present possession, and the patience that pleads day and night until it is revealed. The timeliness of God's long-suffering is witnessed by the triumphant but patient faith of His waiting child.

The great danger in this school of delayed answers is the temptation to think that it may not be God's will to give us what we ask. But if our prayer is according to God's Word and under the leading of the Spirit, we must not give in to such fear. Learn to give God time: time in your daily fellowship with Him, time to exercise the influence of His presence; time to prove its reality. He will lead us from faith to vision; we *shall see* the glory of God.

Let no delay shake your faith. Faith says: First the blade, then the ear, then the full corn in the ear. Each believing prayer is a step nearer the final victory. Each believing prayer helps to ripen the fruit and bring us nearer to it; it fills up the measure of prayer and faith known to God alone; it conquers the hindrances in the unseen world; it hastens the end.

Child of God, give your Father time. He is long-suffering over you. He wants the blessing to be rich, full, and sure. Give Him time, even while you cry unto Him day and night. Remember the word, "Will not God bring about justice for his chosen ones, who cry out to him day and night? Will he keep putting them off? I tell you, he will see that they get justice, and quickly."

The blessing of persevering prayer is unsurpassed. There is nothing as heart-searching as the prayer of faith. It teaches us to discover and confess and give up everything that hinders the answer. It leads to closer fellowship with Him who alone teaches us to pray; it calls us to a closer abiding in Christ alone.

God will perfect that which concerns you. Whether we labor in our daily work or in prayer, time and effort are needed; we must give ourselves to it. Nature reveals her secrets and yields her treasures over time and in season. It is the same in the spiritual realm: the seeds we sow in the soil of heaven require our time and effort, our faith and diligence. Let us give ourselves to prayer. In due season we shall reap, if we faint not.

Let us learn a lesson as we pray for the church of Christ: She is as the poor widow; in the absence of her Lord she is at the mercy of her adversary. Let us ask Him to visit her with the mighty working of His Spirit to prepare her for His coming.

Praying always and not fainting will bring the answer. Keep calling unto Him day and night, and give God time to fulfill your request. He does hear and he does answer.

O Lord my God, teach me to know your way and in faith to understand what your beloved Son has taught us: "He will see that they get justice, and quickly." Let your tender love and the delight you have in hearing and blessing your children lead me to accept your promise—that we receive what we believe, that we have the petitions we ask, and that the answer will in due time be revealed.

Lord, I understand the seasons in nature, and I know to wait with patience for the desired fruit. Fill me with assurance that neither will you delay a moment longer than is needed, and that my faith will hasten the answer.

Blessed Master, you have told us that it is a sign of God's elect that they cry day and night. Teach me to understand this. You know how quickly I grow faint and weary. I feel like you are beyond the need or the reach of continued supplication and that it does not become me to be too insistent. And so, Lord, teach me how real the labor of prayer is. I know that when I have failed at an undertaking in my daily work, I can often succeed by renewed and continuing effort or by giving a problem more time and thought. Show me how by giving myself more entirely to prayer I can obtain what I ask.

Above all, blessed Teacher, Author and Perfecter

of our faith, by your grace and mercy let my whole life be one of trust in the Son of God, who loved me and gave himself for me—in whom my prayer gains acceptance, in whom I have the assurance of the answer. Lord Jesus, in this faith I will always pray and not give up. Amen.

Chapter 6

The All-Prevailing Prayer

"And I will do whatever you ask in my name, so that the Son may bring glory to the Father. You may ask me for anything in my name, and I will do it. Then the Father will give you whatever you ask in my name. I tell you the truth, my Father will give you whatever you ask in my name. Until now you have not asked for anything in my name. Ask and you will receive, and your joy will be complete. In that day you will ask in my name."

John 14:13–14; 15:16; 16:23–24, 26

Until this time the disciples had not asked for anything in the name of Christ, nor had He ever used the expression among them. The closest they came to the thought was that they met together *in His name*. Here in His parting words, before He is betrayed, Jesus repeats the word *whatever* in connection with His promises concerning answered prayer to teach them and us that His name is our only and all-sufficient plea. The power of prayer and the answer depend on the right use of the name.

What is a person's name? It is the title by which a person is represented to us. When I mention or hear a name, it brings to mind the whole person, what I know of him or her, including the impression the person has made on me. The name of a king includes his honor, his power, his kingdom. His name is the symbol of his power.

Each name of God embodies and represents an aspect of the glory of the One who is invisible; and the name of Christ is the expression of all He has done for us and will do as our Mediator.

What is it to take action in the name of another? It is to come with the power of attorney for that person, as his representative and substitute. Use of another's name supposes a mutual trust; no one would give someone else free use of his name without first being assured that his honor and interest were as safe with that person as with himself.

What does it mean when Jesus gives us access

to His name with the assurance that whatever we ask in it will be given to us? To compare a person giving someone else, on a particular occasion, the liberty to ask something in his name is insufficient here, for Jesus gives to *all* His disciples general and unlimited use of His name at *all* times for *anything* they desire. He would not do this if He did not trust us with His interests, if He did not know His honor would be safe in our hands. The free use of the name of another is a token of great confidence, even intimacy. The one who gives his name to another steps aside and allows the other to act for him; the one who takes the name of another gives up his own. When I go in the name of another, I deny myself, taking not only the name but the identity of that one instead of my own.

Such use of a person's name may be by virtue of a *legal arrangement*. A businessman leaving town temporarily gives his manager power of attorney by which he can draw or deposit thousands of dollars in the employer's name. The manager does not make these transactions for himself but in the name of his employer in the interest of the business. It is because the owner knows and trusts his employee as devoted to his interests and business that he dares to put his name and property under his care.

When the Lord Jesus returned to heaven, He left His work—the management of His kingdom on earth—in the hands of His followers. He gave them His name by which to draw all the supplies they needed to conduct His business. They have the spiritual power to avail themselves of the name of Jesus to the extent to which they yield themselves to live for the interests and work of the Master. The use of the name assumes the surrender of interests to the One we represent.

Use of a name may also be by virtue of a *life union*. In the case of the businessman and his manager, the union is temporary. Other arrangements are of a more permanent nature. A child, for example, carries his father's name. The child of a father of good character is sometimes honored or helped by others because of the name he bears. But this kind of favor would not last long if it were discovered that the father's character was questionable. The name and the character must be in harmony.

So it is with Jesus and the believer. We are one; we have one life, one Spirit with Him; for this reason we may come in His name. The power we have in using that name, whether with God, men, or demons, *depends on the measure of our life-union with Him.* So it is more than glibly repeating a name at the end of a prayer—it is using the name that means more to us than life itself.

A common union on earth that empowers one to use a name is in the case of a bride. Whatever station in life she may have had, when she marries and takes the name of her bridegroom, all that he is and owns and represents is hers. She gives up her own name to be called by his, and she receives the full right to use it. She may make purchases in his name, or conduct other business, and not be refused. The bridegroom has chosen her for himself, and counts on her to care for his interests; the two have become one.

The heavenly Bridegroom can do nothing less; having loved us and made us one with himself, He gives those who bear His name the right to present it before the Father with all authority. There is no one who abandons himself to live by the name of Jesus who does not receive in ever-increasing measure the spiritual capacity to ask and receive in that name whatever he will. The bearing of the name of another supposes my having given up my own reputation, and with it my own independent life; but then I have also taken possession of all there is in connection with that name.

These illustrations show the flaws of the common view of a messenger sent to ask in the name of another, or a guilty one appealing to the name of a guarantor. Jesus himself is with the Father; it is not an absentee in whose name we pray. Even when we pray to Jesus himself, it must be in His name. The name represents the person; to ask in His name is to ask in full union of interest, life, and love as one who lives in and for Him.

If the name of Jesus has undivided supremacy in my heart and life, my faith will gain the assurance that what I ask in that name cannot be refused. The name and the power of asking go hand in hand; when the name of Jesus has become the power that rules my life, power in prayer with God will be evident as well.

Everything depends on our relationship to the name; the power it has on my life is the power it will have in my prayers. There is more than one expression in Scripture that can make this clear to us. When we *do all* in the name of the Lord Jesus, we can *ask all*.

When we read, "We shall walk in the name of our God," we see that the power of the name must rule in the whole life; only then will we have power in prayer. God looks not at the lips but at the life to see what the name means to us. When Scripture speaks of "men who have given their lives for the name of the Lord Jesus," or of one "ready to die for the name," we see what our relationship to His name must be; when it is everything *to* me, it will obtain everything *for* me. If I let it have all I have, it will let me have all it has.

"And I will do whatever you ask in my name." Jesus means the promise literally. Christians have sought to limit it—it looks too simple; it is hardly safe to trust man so unconditionally. However, the condition "in my name" is its own safeguard. It is a spiritual power that no one can use further than he obtains the capacity for by his living and acting in that name. As we bear that name before men, we have power to use it before God.

We must ask God's Holy Spirit to show us what the name means and what the proper use of it is. It is through the Spirit that the name, which is above every name in heaven, will take the place of supremacy in our heart and life.

Disciples of Jesus, allow the lessons of this day

to enter deep into your hearts. The Master says, "The Father will give you whatever you ask in my name."

Heaven is open to you; the treasures and powers of the world of the spirit are placed at your disposal on behalf of those around you. Learn to pray in the name of Jesus. Just as He said to the disciples, He says to us, "Until now you have not asked for anything in my name. Ask and you will receive, and your joy will be complete."

Let each disciple of Jesus seek to avail himself of the rights of his royal priesthood and use the power placed at his disposal. Let Christians awake and hear the message: your prayer can obtain what otherwise will be withheld and can accomplish what otherwise would remain undone. Arise and use the name of Jesus to open the treasures of heaven for this perishing world. Learn as the servants of the King to use His name.

Blessed Lord, it is as if each lesson you give has such fullness and depth of meaning that I think if I can only learn this one, I will know how to pray. Today I feel again as if I need only one prayer: Teach me what it is to pray in your name. Teach me to live and act, to walk and speak, all in the name of Jesus that my prayer cannot be anything else but in that blessed name.

And teach me, Lord, to hold to the precious promise that whatever *we ask in your name, you will do. I do not yet fully understand it, nor have I fully attained to the wondrous union you meant when you said* "in my name," *yet I would hold fast the promise until it fills my heart with the unwavering assurance—anything in the name of Jesus.*

Teach me this by your Holy Spirit. You said of Him, "The Father will send the Comforter, in my name." He knows what it is to honor the power of that name, to use that name alone and so to glorify you. Lord Jesus, allow your Spirit to dwell in me and fill me. I yield my whole being to His rule and leading. Your name and your Spirit are one; through Him your name will be the strength of my life and my prayer. I will speak to others and prove that this is indeed the name above every name. Teach me to pray in your name. Amen.

Chapter 7

The Holy Spirit and Prayer

"In that day you will no longer ask me anything. I tell you the truth, my Father will give you whatever you ask in my name. Until now you have not asked for anything in my name. Ask and you will receive, and your joy will be complete. Though I have been speaking figuratively, a time is coming when I will no longer use this kind of language but will tell you plainly about my Father. In that day you will ask in my name. I am not saying that I will ask the Father on your behalf."

John 16:23–26

But you, dear friends, build yourselves up in your most holy faith and pray in the Holy Spirit. Keep yourselves in God's love as you wait for the mercy of our Lord Jesus Christ to bring you to eternal life. Praying in the Holy Spirit, keep yourselves in the love of God.

Jude 20–21

The words of John (1 John 2:12–14) to little children, to young men, and to fathers, suggest that there are in the Christian life three main stages of experience: The *first,* that of the newborn child, with the assurance and the joy of forgiveness. The *second,* the transition stage of struggle and growth in knowledge and strength; young men growing strong, God's Word doing its work in them and giving them victory over the evil one. And then the *final* stage of maturity and ripeness: the fathers, who have entered deeply into the knowledge and fellowship of the Eternal One.

In Christ's teaching there also appear to be three stages in the prayer life, somewhat analogous. In the Sermon on the Mount we have the initial stage; in it, His teaching is comprised all in one word: *Father.* Pray to your Father; your Father sees, hears, knows, and will reward much more than any earthly father! Only be childlike and trustful.

Later on comes something like the transitional stage of conflict and conquest, in words like these: "This kind goes out only by fasting and prayer" and "Shall not God avenge his own elect who cry day and night unto him?"

Finally, we have in His parting words a higher level. The children have become men; they are now the Master's friends, from whom He keeps no secrets, and to whom He says, "All things that I have heard from my Father I have made known unto you." To these, in the oft-repeated "whatever you desire," He hands over the keys to the kingdom. Now the time has come for the power of prayer in His name to be put to the test.

The contrast between this final stage and the previous preparatory ones is marked distinctly in the words we are to meditate on: "Until now you have not asked for anything in my name"; "In that day you will ask in my name." We know what "in that day" means. It is the day of the outpouring of the Holy Spirit.

The great work Christ was to do on the cross, the mighty power and victory manifested in His resurrection and ascension, were to culminate in the outpouring as never before of the glory of God. The Spirit of the glorified Jesus was to be the life of His disciples. One of the marks of that Spirit-dispensation was to be a power in prayer previously unknown: prayer in the name of Jesus—asking and obtaining whatever they would as a manifestation of the Spirit's indwelling.

To understand how the coming of the Holy Spirit was to open up a new dimension in prayer, we must remember who He is, what His work is, and the significance of His not being given until Jesus was glorified. It is in the Spirit that God exists, for He is Spirit. It is in the Spirit that the Son was begotten of the Father; it is in the fellowship of the Spirit that the Father and the Son are one. It is through the Spirit that this communion of life and love is maintained—the eternal giving to the Son, which is the Father's prerogative, and the eternal asking and receiving, which is the Son's right. It has been so from all eternity. It is especially so now, when the Son as Mediator ever lives to pray and intercede.

The great work that Jesus began on earth of reconciling God and man, He carries on in heaven. To accomplish this, He took into His own person the conflict between God's righteousness and our sin. On the cross, in His own body, He once for all ended the struggle. Then He ascended to heaven in order that He might through His people continue to carry out the deliverance and manifest the victory He had obtained. For this purpose He ever lives to pray; in His unceasing intercession He places himself in living fellowship with the unceasing prayer of His redeemed ones. In fact, it is His unceasing intercession that reveals itself in their prayers and gives them a power they never had before.

Christ does this through the Holy Spirit. The Spirit of the glorified Jesus had not come (John 7:39), and could not, until Jesus had been glorified. This gift of the Father was something distinctively new, entirely different from what the Old Testament saints had known. Christ's entrance within the veil, the redemption of our human nature into fellowship with His power and glory, and the union of our humanity in Christ with the triune God were of such inconceivable significance that the Holy Spirit, who had come from Christ's exalted humanity to testify in our hearts of what Christ had accomplished, was indeed no longer only what He had been in the Old Testament.

It was literally true that the Holy Spirit was "not yet," for Christ was not yet glorified. He came first as the Spirit of the glorified Jesus. The Son, who was from eternity God, had entered upon a new existence as man, and returned to heaven with a glory He did not have before. So also the blessed Spirit, whom the Son, upon His ascension, received from the Father (Acts 2:33) into His glorified humanity, came to us with new life He had not previously been able to give. Under the Old Testament, He was invoked as the Spirit of God; at Pentecost, He descended as the Spirit of the glorified Jesus, bringing down and communicating to us the full fruit and power of the accomplished redemption.

The continued efficacy and application of our redemption is maintained in the intercession of Christ. And it is through the Holy Spirit descending from Christ to us that we are drawn up into the great stream of His ever-ascending prayers. The Spirit prays for us without words. In the depths of our hearts, where even our thoughts are at times without form, the Spirit takes us up into the wonderful flow of the life of the triune God. Through the Spirit, Christ's prayers become ours, and ours are made His; we ask what we will, and it is given to us. We will then understand from experience that we have not really asked before. Now we can ask.

Pray in the name of Christ that your joy may be full. This comes through the baptism of the Holy Spirit. This is more than the Spirit of God of the Old Testament. This is more than the Spirit of conversion and regeneration the disciples knew before Pentecost. This is more than the Spirit with a measure of His influence and working. This is the Holy Spirit, the Spirit of the glorified Jesus in His exaltation-power, coming as the Spirit of the indwelling Jesus, revealing the Son and the Father within (John 14:16–23).

When this Spirit is the Spirit not only of hours of prayer but of our whole life and walk, when He glorifies Jesus in us by revealing the completeness of His work and by making us wholly one with Him and like Him, then we can truly pray in His name, because we are indeed one with Him. Then we have immediate access to the Father of which Jesus says, "I am not saying that I will ask the Father on your behalf." We need to understand and believe that to be filled with the Spirit of the glorified One is the one need of God's believing people. Then we will understand what it is to "pray in the Spirit on all occasions with all kinds of prayers and requests" (Ephesians 6:18), and what it is to pray in the Holy Spirit and to keep ourselves in the love of God. "In that day you will ask in my name."

What our prayer avails depends upon what we are and what our life is. Living in the name of

Christ is the secret of praying in the name of Christ; living in the Spirit equips us for praying in the Spirit. Abiding in Christ gives us the right and power to ask whatever we will; the extent of our abiding is the extent of our power in prayer.

It is the Spirit dwelling within us that prays, not always in actual words and thoughts but in a way that is deeper than utterance. To the degree that Christ's Spirit is in us so is our prayer genuine.

Let our lives be full of Christ and full of His Spirit, and the wonderfully unlimited promises concerning prayer will no longer appear out of reach.

O God, in holy awe I bow before you, the triune One. Again I have seen how the mystery of prayer is the mystery of the Trinity. I adore the Father who always hears us and the Son who always prays for us. I adore the Holy Spirit, who lifts us up into the fellowship of that ever-blessed, never-ceasing exchange of asking and receiving. I bow, my God, in adoring worship, before the infinite condescension that through the Holy Spirit takes us and our prayers into the divine fellowship of love.

My blessed Lord Jesus, help me to understand

your teaching that it is the indwelling Spirit, united with you, pouring from you, who is the Spirit of prayer. Teach me to become an empty, wholly consecrated vessel yielded to His leading. Teach me to honor and trust Him as a living person, for that He is. Teach me especially in prayer to wait in silence and give Him place to breathe within me His unutterable intercession.

Teach me that through Him it is possible to pray without ceasing and to pray without failing because He makes me a partaker of the never-ceasing, never-failing intercession in which you, the Son, appear before the Father. Lord, fulfill in me your promises concerning prayer. Amen.

Chapter 8

Christ the Intercessor

*"But I have prayed for you . . . that your
faith may not fail."*

Luke 22:32

*"In that day you will ask in my name. I am not
saying that I will ask the Father on your behalf."*

John 16:26

*Therefore he is able to save completely those who
come to God through him, because he always
lives to intercede for them.*

Hebrews 7:25

All growth in the spiritual life is dependent upon
clearer insight into what Jesus is to us. The more
I realize that Christ must be everything to me and
that all in Christ is for me, the more I learn to

live the real life of faith—dying to self, and living wholly in Christ. The Christian life is no longer a vain struggle to live aright but rather resting in Christ and finding Him as my life. This is especially true in the life of prayer.

Prayer also comes under the law of faith, and when seen in the light of the fullness and completeness that is in Jesus, the believer understands that prayer no longer needs to be a matter of strain or anxious care; it is an experience of what Christ will do for us and in us—a participation in the life of Christ, which as on earth so in heaven, ascends to the Father as prayer. He can begin to pray not only trusting in the merits of Jesus or in the intercession by which our unworthy prayers are made acceptable, but in that union in which He prays in us and we in Him.

The whole of salvation is Christ himself: He has given *himself* to us; He lives in us. Because He prays, we pray. Just as the disciples asked Jesus, when they saw Him pray, to teach them, so we, now that He is our Intercessor, want Him to teach us and make us participators with him in the life of prayer.

This is illustrated clearly on the last night of His life on earth. In His high-priestly prayer

(John 17), He shows us how and what He prays to the Father and what He will pray when once ascended to heaven. Yet in His parting address He repeatedly associated His going to the Father with the disciples' new life of prayer. The two would be ultimately connected; His entrance into the work of His eternal intercession *would be the beginning and the power of their new prayer life in His name.* A vision of Jesus interceding for us gives us courage to pray in His name.

To understand this, think first of His intercession—He lives to intercede for us. The work of Christ on earth as Priest was but the beginning— as Aaron, He shed His blood; as Melchizedek, He lives within the veil to continue His work in the power of eternal life.

As Melchizedek is more glorious than Aaron, so in intercession the atonement has its true power and glory. It is Christ who died and is at the right hand of God, making intercession for us. That intercession is a reality, a work that is absolutely necessary and without which the continued application of redemption cannot take place.

In the incarnation and resurrection of Jesus, the wondrous reconciliation took place; man became partaker of the divine life. But the personal appropriation of this reconciliation in each of His members here below cannot take place without the unceasing exercise of divine power by the Head in heaven. In all conversion and sanctification, in every victory over sin and the world, there is a manifestation of the power of God.

This exercise of His power takes place only through His prayers. He asks the Father and receives from the Father. He is able to save because He ever lives to intercede. There is no need of His people that He conveys in intercession that the Godhead can deny: His mediation on the throne is as real and indispensable as the cross. Nothing takes place without His intercession. It engages all His being and power; it is His unceasing occupation at the right hand of the Father.

We participate not only in the benefits of His work but in the work itself because we are His body. The body and its members are one: "The eye cannot say to the hand, 'I don't need you!' And the head cannot say to the feet, 'I don't need you!'" (1 Corinthians 12:21). We share with Jesus in all He is and has. We are partakers of His life, His righteousness, His work. We share with Him in His intercession as well; it is not a work He does without us.

We do this because we are partakers of His life: Christ is our life; Christ lives in us. The life in Him and in us is one and the same. His life in heaven is a life of prayer. When His life takes possession of us, it does not lose its character; it is a life of prayer that without ceasing asks and receives from God.

Do not think mistakenly that there are two separate currents of prayer rising upward, one from Him and one from His people. Our life-union with Him is also a prayer-union; what He prays joins with what we pray. He is as the angel with the golden censer. Unto him was given much incense, the secret of acceptable prayer, that he should add it unto the prayers of all the saints upon the golden altar. We live and abide in the Interceding One.

The Only-begotten is the only one who has the true right to pray; to Him alone it was said, "Ask, and it shall be given thee." As in all other things, the fullness dwells in Him, including true prayerfulness. He alone has the power of prayer.

Growth in our spiritual life involves a clearer insight into all the treasures that are *in Him.*

Faith in the intercession of Jesus must not only be that He prays on our behalf when we do not or cannot pray, but that as the Author of our life and our faith, He enables us to pray in unison with Him. Our prayer must be a work of faith. As Jesus communicates His whole life to us, He also breathes His prayers into ours.

It is a new level in a believer's spiritual life when he realizes how truly and entirely Christ is his life, standing as guarantor for His faithful and obedient ones. It is then that the believer truly begins to live the life of faith.

No less blessed will be the discovery that Christ is the keeper of our prayer life too, the center and embodiment of all prayer, which is communicated by Him through the Holy Spirit to the throne. He lives forever to make intercession as the Head of the body, as the leader in that new and living way, which He has opened up as the Author and the Perfecter of our faith.

He provides for everything in the life of His redeemed ones by living and praying through them. He prays for us not to render our faith unnecessary, but so that our faith does not fail; our faith and prayers of faith are rooted in His.

If we abide in the ever-living Intercessor,

praying with and through Him, we may ask whatever we wish and it will be done for us.

All these wonderful prayer promises have as their aim and justification the glory of God in the manifestation of His kingdom and the salvation of sinners. As long as we pray primarily for ourselves, the promises of His final night on earth will remain a sealed book to us. The promises are to the fruit-bearing branches of the Vine; they are for the disciples sent into the world to live for the lost and perishing; they are for His faithful servants and intimate friends who take up the work He left behind, who, like their Lord, have become as the grain of wheat or kernel of corn, losing their life in order to multiply it a hundredfold; to these the promises are given.

Each of us must find out what our work is to be and what souls are entrusted to our prayers. Let us make our intercession for them our life of fellowship with God, and we shall not only find the promises of power in prayer made true for us, but we shall also begin to realize how our abiding in Christ and His abiding in us allows us to share in His joy and blessing to the saving of souls.

We not only owe everything to His intercession, but we are taken up as active partners in it.

Now we understand what it is to pray in the name of Jesus and why it has such power—in His name, through His Spirit, in perfect union with himself. When will we be convinced of our part in this intercession of Christ and begin to pray in faith?

Blessed Lord, in humble adoration I would again bow before you. Your whole redemptive work has now passed into prayer; all that now occupies you in maintaining and dispensing what you purchased with your blood is prayer. You ever live to pray. Because we are in you and direct access to the Father is always open, our life can be one of unceasing prayer; the answer to our prayer is sure.

O Lord, you have invited your people to be your fellow-workers in a life of prayer. You have united yourself with your body that they might share with you in the ministry of intercession; through this alone the world will be filled with the fruit of your redemption and the glory of the Father. With more liberty than ever before I come to you, Lord, and ask you to teach me to pray. Yours is a life of prayer. Your life is mine.

Help me to know, as did your disciples, that you are in the Father and I am in you and you in me.

May the uniting power of the Holy Spirit make my life one of abiding in you and your intercession; let my prayer be its echo, that the Father may hear me. Lord Jesus, may the mind of Christ be in me. So shall I be prepared to be the channel through which your intercession can flow and pour its blessing on all the world. Amen.

More Classic Andrew Murray
Edited Especially for *Today's* Readers

Humility: In twelve brief but powerful chapters Andrew Murray takes readers on a journey through Scripture and Christ's life, showing us the utmost need for humility—as opposed to pride—in the Christian life. Demonstrating for us what Christ did when he took the form of a servant, Murray calls humility a distinguishing characteristic of the believer and encourages us to embrace this attitude in our own lives.

The Ministry of Intercessory Prayer: Murray offers practical, biblical instruction in intercessory prayer as well as a 31-day course, "Pray Without Ceasing," at the end of the book. All of this is part of his simple but profound goal to change the world through intercession.

Abiding in Christ: Using the image of the vine and the branches to explain the concept of abiding in Christ, Murray offers a message as timely now as it was a century ago. He urges readers to yield themselves to Jesus in order to know "the full blessedness of abiding in Christ."

BETHANYHOUSE